Double Take

By John Escott

Chapter 1

There was someone watching her.

Rosie knew this quite suddenly. She turned.

Behind her on the platform at Waterloo Station was another girl. Rosie could see why the other girl was staring at her.

The other girl smiled.

"I'm supposed to be going to Carnmouth, too," said the other girl. "I've got to meet my father."

"Then we'll be on the same train," Rosie said.

The other girl was trying to make up her mind about something.

"How would you like to travel first class?" she said. "You could have my ticket. I want to go to a party tonight, then travel down tomorrow."

Why not use your ticket tomorrow?

"I *could* use my ticket tomorrow," the other girl agreed. "But I was hoping you'd do me a favour. We look a bit alike, don't we? That's what gave me the idea."

"What idea?" Rosie said.

"Could you tell your friend you're coming tomorrow, instead?"

"Well ... I suppose I could," Rosie said. "But why?"

"To help me out. I'm booked in at the Royal Palace Hotel, so you could stay there tonight. I'm told it's very nice."

Rosie knew the Royal Palace Hotel at Carnmouth. It was a huge, white hotel on the cliff top. You had to be rich to stay there.

"My father won't get there until tomorrow afternoon," the other girl went on. "I'll be there by then. And if you wear sunglasses and leave in the morning, nobody will realize there were two of us."

"But why do you need somebody to take your place tonight?" Rosie asked.

"Because if I don't arrive until tomorrow, they might tell my father."

"And you don't want him to know about the party," Rosie said.

"That's right."

"What's your name?" Rosie asked.

"Jessica Grover," the other girl said. "What's yours?"

"Rosie Caldwell."

Will you do it, Rosie? Will you change places with me, just for twenty-four hours?

Rosie was always game for a laugh.

"OK," she said, grinning.

9

Chapter 2

The woman behind the desk at the Royal
Palace Hotel smiled.

The porter picked up Rosie's sports
bag. They took the lift to the third floor.
Then the porter led the way to the room.

Room 33 was large. Rosie could see the sea through the window.

"Lunch is served in the restaurant between 12 noon and 2 o'clock," the young porter said. "You can get sandwiches and other snacks in the bar at any time. And there is also Room Service."

"Room Service," Rosie repeated. "Oh."

"Would you like something, Miss?" the porter asked.

Having something in her room would be better than eating in the restaurant, Rosie thought. No one would see her. "Can I have some sandwiches?" she said.

"Thank you. Will that be all, miss?"

"Er – can you make a phone call for me?" Rosie said. "There won't be anyone there now, but you can leave a message on the answering machine."

The young man looked surprised. "Certainly, Miss," he said.

Rosie gave him the telephone number.

Just say that Rosie is OK but won't be arriving until tomorrow.

The young man dialled the number and spoke into the phone. Rosie smiled at him. "Thanks. My friend asked me to leave that message."

"I see, Miss," said the young man, putting down the phone.

He seemed to be waiting for something.

After a moment, Rosie realized what it was. She found a fifty-pence piece. "Thank you," she said, putting the coin into his hand.

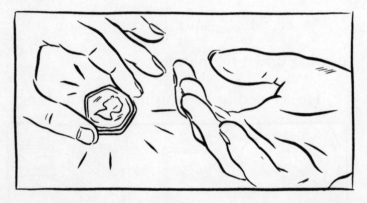

He went out, closing the door behind him.

A few minutes later, Rosie opened the door again, so that she would see when her sandwiches came.

I'm going to like it here, she thought, smiling.

Chapter 3

That afternoon, Rosie used the swimming pool.

The waiter brought her a strawberry sundae and a long cold drink.

This is the life!

Nobody spoke to her except the waiter. Nobody seemed to take much notice of her at all. It was perfect.

That evening Rosie had dinner in the hotel restaurant. She sat at a table in a corner. She ate roast duck, followed by banana split, then coffee. She wondered if Jessica Grover was enjoying her party.

There was a newspaper on a nearby table. It was the Carnmouth Evening Echo. Rosie noticed a small headline on the front page:

She read the report under it. It said that the important visitor was a millionaire. His name was Sir Mervyn Grover.

So that's who Jessica's father is, Rosie thought. No wonder she can stay at places like this!

Chapter 4

Rosie was eating her breakfast the next morning when the woman from the hotel desk came across to her table.

Miss Grover, your car has arrived to take you sightseeing.

Rosie stared at her. "Oh," she said. Jessica hadn't told her about this. Still, it might be fun. Rosie finished her coffee and

followed the woman into the lobby.
Another woman was waiting there.

For a moment, Rosie panicked. Did
this woman know the real Jessica?

Your father thought you might enjoy a little sightseeing tour this morning, just to pass the time until he arrives later.

The car is right here.

Thank you.

Afterwards, Rosie wondered why she hadn't suspected something at once. But the woman seemed nice and friendly. Maybe Jessica did things like this all the time, Rosie thought.

But she did start to worry when they drove through the town and out on to a country road. No one said a word.

Where are we going?

You'll see.

The woman wasn't smiling now. She kept looking out of the rear window. She

seemed worried somebody might be

following them.

Chapter 5

It was almost an hour before the car turned off a narrow lane and through some open gates.

"We're here," the woman told Rosie.

"Now what?" Rosie asked.

The woman smiled. It wasn't a nice smile.

We send a little message to your daddy. A million-pound message.

"You're asking for a million pounds?" Rosie said. "For me? You think he'll pay it?"

"He'll pay," the woman said. The car stopped and she opened the door. "Get out."

Rosie looked around. She saw an old farmhouse. Then a door opened and a man came out. He was big and fat and was smoking a cigar.

"Good morning, Miss Grover," he said.

"I'm not Miss Grover," Rosie said.

"I'm Rosie Caldwell."

And at that moment, three cars came round the corner of the house.

They were police cars.

"How did you know?" one of the policemen asked Rosie, as they drove back towards Carnmouth.

"I watched the woman ask the way at the filling station," Rosie said. "She thought she was safe because I couldn't hear her."

"Wasn't she safe?" the policeman said.

"No," Rosie said. "You see ... I'm deaf. But I can lip read."

The policeman smiled. "I see. And you aren't Jessica Grover, the millionaire's daughter?"

"No," Rosie said. "And if this is what it's like being a millionaire's daughter, then I'm glad I'm not!"

But who are you, and how did you come to be staying at the Royal Palace Hotel?

It's a long story ...